PLYMOUTH DISTRICT LIBRARY

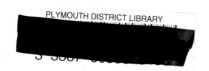

D1716664

J 551.6 M

What are weather
and climate? /

Plymouth District Library
223 S. Main St.
Plymouth, MI 48170
May 2015

J 551.6 M

WHAT ARE WEATHER AND CLIMATE?

JOANNE MATTERN

Britannica®
Educational Publishing

IN ASSOCIATION WITH

ROSEN
EDUCATIONAL SERVICES

Published in 2015 by Britannica Educational Publishing (a trademark of Encyclopædia Britannica, Inc.) in association with The Rosen Publishing Group, Inc.
29 East 21st Street, New York, NY 10010

Copyright © 2015 The Rosen Publishing Group, Inc., and Encyclopædia Britannica, Inc. Encyclopaedia Britannica, Britannica, and the Thistle logo are registered trademarks of Encyclopædia Britannica, Inc. All rights reserved.

Distributed exclusively by Rosen Publishing.
To see additional Britannica Educational Publishing titles, go to rosenpublishing.com.

First Edition

Britannica Educational Publishing
J. E. Luebering: Director, Core Reference Group
Mary Rose McCudden: Editor, Britannica Student Encyclopedia

Rosen Publishing
Hope Lourie Killcoyne: Executive Editor
Natalie Regis: Editor
Nelson Sá: Art Director
Michael Moy: Designer
Cindy Reiman: Photography Manager

Library of Congress Cataloging-in-Publication Data

Mattern, Joanne, 1963–
What are weather and climate?/Joanne Mattern.—First edition.
    pages cm—(Let's find out! Weather)
Includes bibliographical references and index.
Audience: 3–6.
ISBN 978-1-62275-779-4 (library bound) — ISBN 978-1-62275-780-0 (pbk.) —
ISBN 978-1-62275-781-7 (6-pack)
1. Weather—Juvenile literature. 2. Meteorology—Juvenile literature. I. Title.
QC981.3.M38 2015
551.6—dc23
2014027237

Manufactured in the United States of America

Photo Credits
Cover background, p. 1, interior pages background © iStockphoto.com/Bartosz Hadyniak; cover inset from left Galyna Andrushko/Shutterstock.com, Mykola Mazuryk/Shutterstock.com, Denis Burdin/Shutterstock.com; p. 4 © iStockphoto.com/Mari; p. 5 © Philip Coblentz/Digital Vision/Getty Images; pp. 6, 7, 8, 9, 10, 11, 15, 16, 18, 23 Encyclopædia Britannica, Inc.; p. 12 Chris Cross/Caiaimage/Getty Images; p. 13 Ryszard Stelmachowicz/Shutterstock.com; p. 14 Gary Hincks/Science Source; p. 17 Josef Friedhuber/iStock/Thinkstock; p. 19 Rich Carey/Shutterstock.com; p. 20 Jessica Wilson/NASA/Science Source; p. 21 Narinder Nanu/AFP/Getty Images; p. 22 karamysh/Shutterstock.com; p. 24 Adisa/Shutterstock.com; p. 25 NOAA; p. 26 Volodymyr Goinyk/Shutterstock.com; p. 27 Sakkawokkie/iStock/Thinkstock; pp. 28–29 © Sergiy Serdyuk/Fotolia; p. 29 © AP Images.

CONTENTS

WEATHER AND CLIMATE

Look outside. What is the weather like today? Is it sunny or cloudy? Is it hot or cold? Weather is the daily state of the atmosphere, or air, in any given place. Weather is made up of specific conditions. These include temperature, wind speed and direction, and precipitation. Weather conditions affect the comfort, food supply, and safety of people in all parts of the world.

Water that falls to the ground is precipitation. Rain is one type of precipitation.

The climate in this location is mostly warm.

Climate is not the same as weather. Climate is the average of weather conditions in an area over a long period of time. Weather can change from day to day or even hour to hour. It also changes with the seasons. In the winter an area may be cold and snowy, but in the summer that same area can be hot and humid. Climate does not change so quickly. An area's climate is what the weather is like there most of the time, even when it changes with the seasons. The seasons have roughly the same conditions from year to year in a particular climate.

THINK ABOUT IT

What are some ways that weather affects your daily life?

What Causes Weather?

Some aspects of weather are easy to notice. You can feel the temperature, which is how hot or cold it is outside. You can also feel the wind blowing. You know when it is raining or snowing, too. Other weather conditions are not as noticeable. These include humidity and air pressure. Whether you can feel them or not, all of these conditions together make up the weather.

The heat of the Sun causes wind. It heats the tropical zone more than polar regions.

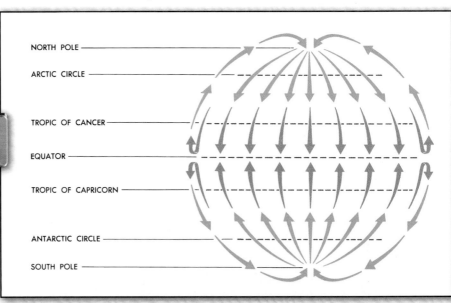

NORTH POLE

ARCTIC CIRCLE

TROPIC OF CANCER

EQUATOR

TROPIC OF CAPRICORN

ANTARCTIC CIRCLE

SOUTH POLE

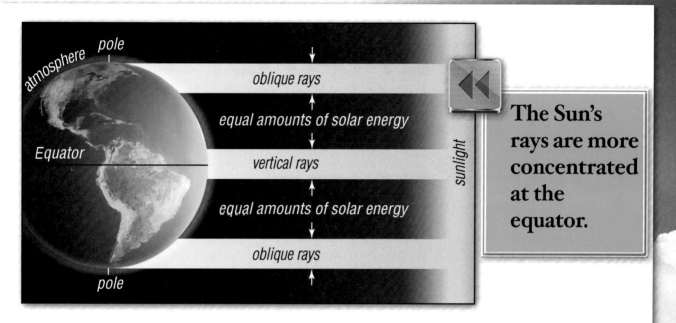

atmosphere
pole
oblique rays
equal amounts of solar energy
Equator
vertical rays
equal amounts of solar energy
oblique rays
pole
sunlight

The Sun's rays are more concentrated at the equator.

The elements of weather all start with energy from the Sun. The Sun heats the air and the water. But the energy from the Sun does not reach all parts of Earth equally or at the same time. This leads to differences in the weather around the world.

COMPARE AND CONTRAST
Which areas of Earth receive the most direct sunlight and which receive the least sunlight?

TEMPERATURE AND AIR PRESSURE

Many things shape the temperature of a place. One is the amount of direct sunlight a place gets. Another is the type of landforms that are found in a particular place. Some parts of Earth's surface, such as bodies of water, absorb more energy than others. Temperature is also affected by how cloudy a place is. Clouds block some of the Sun's rays during the day. But they can also help keep warm air near the ground at night.

This map shows the average air pressure at sea level in January.

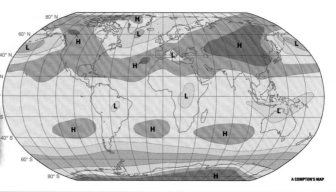

AVERAGE SEA-LEVEL ATMOSPHERIC PRESSURES IN JANUARY

Millibars of Pressure

- Over 1,024
- 1,016 to 1,024
- 1,008 to 1,016
- 1,000 to 1,008
- Under 1,000

H High-Pressure Cell
L Low-Pressure Cell

A COMPTON'S MAP

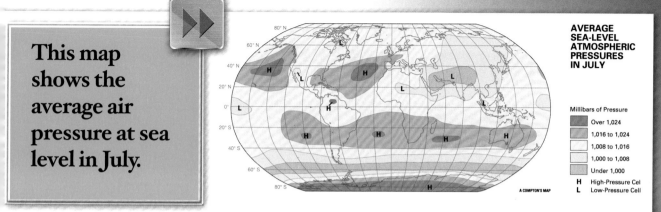

This map shows the average air pressure at sea level in July.

AVERAGE
SEA-LEVEL
ATMOSPHERIC
PRESSURES
IN JULY

Millibars of Pressure

Over 1,024
1,016 to 1,024
1,008 to 1,016
1,000 to 1,008
Under 1,000

H High-Pressure Cell
L Low-Pressure Cell

A COMPTON'S MAP

Differences in heating affect Earth's atmospheric pressure. The air that surrounds Earth is called the atmosphere. Its weight presses down and creates atmospheric pressure. Heat from the Sun causes changes in this pressure. That is because as air is heated it becomes lighter.

Areas of high and low pressure are always moving around the globe. Air in areas of high pressure always moves to areas of low pressure. This causes changes in the weather.

THINK ABOUT IT

If you fill a balloon with air and hold it closed, the air pressure is higher inside the balloon than it is outside. What happens if you let go of the balloon?

WIND AND WATER

Temperature changes also create wind. For example, the Sun heats land and water differently. Air over land is usually warmer than air over the water. As the heated air over the land expands, it becomes lighter and rises. Heavier air from the ocean blows in to take its place. This creates a sea breeze.

By day, the land is warm and the sea is cool. The breeze is off the sea. At night, the land is cool and the sea is warm. The breeze is off the land.

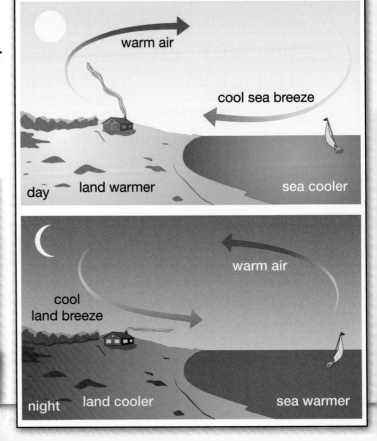

warm air

cool sea breeze

day   land warmer   sea cooler

cool land breeze

warm air

night   land cooler   sea warmer

Winds are named for the direction they come from. For example, a west wind starts in the west and moves east.

Water also plays a part in the weather. Water in oceans, lakes, and rivers evaporates when it is heated by the Sun. This water moves into the air as a gas called water vapor. Humidity is the amount of moisture (that is, the amount

To **evaporate** is to change from a liquid into a gas, or vapor, as a result of being heated.

The Earth's water is constantly being recycled in a process known as the water cycle.

of water vapor stored) in the air. Warm air can hold more water vapor than cold air. That is why it often feels humid in the summer, while the air in the winter feels dry.

As water vapor moves higher into the sky, it cools down. That is because the temperature of the air is generally cooler as one moves away from the surface of Earth. The vapor starts to turn back into a liquid as water droplets. The water droplets together form clouds. When many droplets come together, they form larger, heavier drops. At some point they get too heavy to stay in the cloud and

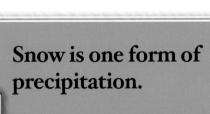

Snow is one form of precipitation.

they fall to Earth as precipitation.

There are many different types of precipitation, depending on the temperature of the air. If the temperature is warm, water droplets in the clouds will fall as rain. If it is cold, the droplets freeze and form snowflakes.

Hail is another type of precipitation. Water can freeze inside of clouds and fall as chunks of ice.

What Is Climate?

Meteorologists keep track of the weather conditions throughout the world. They describe the climate of an area by comparing the measurements of certain conditions over a long time. For example, they have kept track of the temperatures for every day in the last 100 years in Chicago, Illinois. They are able to tell us that the temperatures in September are usually between 57 and 76° Fahrenheit (14–24° Celsius).

This image shows weather fronts. Cold fronts are when cold air pushes up warmer air. Warm fronts are when warm air rises up and over cooler air.

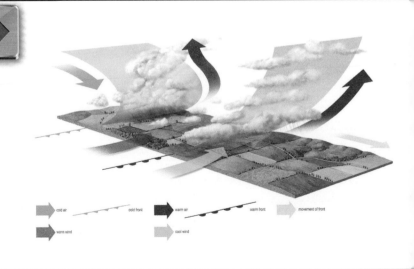

cold air   cold front   warm air   warm front   movement of front

warm wind   cool wind

The weather conditions in an area can change a great deal from year to year, but over a long time patterns can be seen. The patterns show that weather conditions occurring in one part of one year are very similar to weather conditions that occur in other years. The highest and lowest temperatures ever recorded at a site are also important to know. They give an idea of the range of temperatures one might experience in that location.

A **meteorologist** is a scientist who studies the weather.

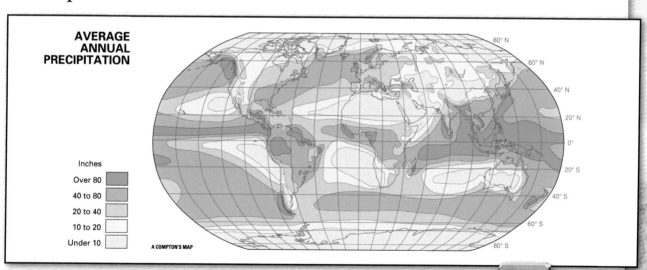

AVERAGE ANNUAL PRECIPITATION

Inches
Over 80
40 to 80
20 to 40
10 to 20
Under 10

A COMPTON'S MAP

80° N
60° N
40° N
20° N
0°
20° S
40° S
60° S
80° S

Meteorologists keep records about weather around the globe. This map shows average yearly precipitation.

LATITUDE

Certain features make the weather in an area the same from year to year. One of those features is the latitude of a place. Lines of latitude (also called parallels) circle Earth parallel to the equator. The lines describe how far

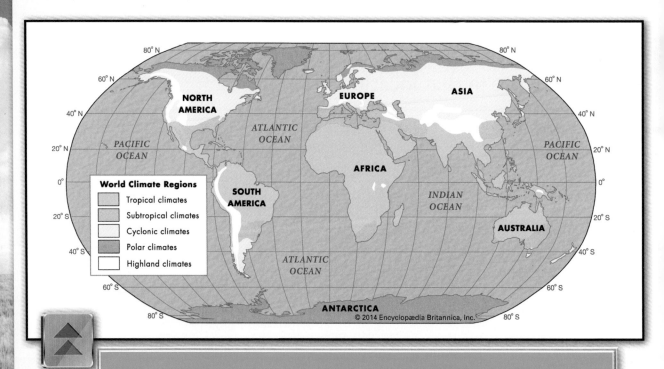

World Climate Regions
- Tropical climates
- Subtropical climates
- Cyclonic climates
- Polar climates
- Highland climates

NORTH AMERICA
EUROPE
ASIA
ATLANTIC OCEAN
PACIFIC OCEAN
PACIFIC OCEAN
AFRICA
SOUTH AMERICA
INDIAN OCEAN
AUSTRALIA
ATLANTIC OCEAN
ANTARCTICA
© 2014 Encyclopædia Britannica, Inc.

80° N · 60° N · 40° N · 20° N · 0° · 20° S · 40° S · 60° S · 80° S

Places along the same lines of latitude generally have similar types of climate.

The polar bear is named for the polar region that is its home.

north or south of the equator a place is located. The latitudes closest to the equator are called the tropics. They are almost always warm because they get direct sunlight all year long. Places that are far away from the equator do not get a lot of direct sunlight. These places, such as the North and South Poles, have cold temperatures.

The **equator** is an imaginary circle around Earth. It divides the planet into two equal halves, with the North Pole at one end and the South Pole at the other end.

OCEANS AND WINDS

Oceans affect climate in several ways. Most of the Sun's heat is absorbed by the oceans. As the oceans warm up, water evaporates and turns into water vapor. The water vapor makes the air warm and wet. Because of this, land near an ocean usually has a milder climate than land away from the ocean.

Ocean currents also play an important role in climate. Winds

About one-third of the Sun's heat is reflected back or gets scattered by the air.

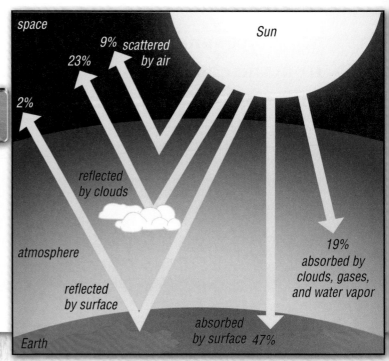

space

Sun

9% scattered by air

23%

2%

reflected by clouds

atmosphere

reflected by surface

19% absorbed by clouds, gases, and water vapor

absorbed by surface 47%

Earth

move warm water from the tropics to the poles and cold water from the poles toward the tropics. Some of the major currents move in set patterns. For example, the Gulf Stream is a collection of currents that flow around the edges of the northern Atlantic Ocean. It brings warm waters to northern areas and colder waters to the south. This keeps cities near the coasts warmer or colder than areas further inland.

This tropical ocean is warm and is home to many different types of sea life.

THINK ABOUT IT
London, in England, is farther north than Chicago, in the United States. London's average temperatures in the winter are often 10° Fahrenheit higher than Chicago's. Why might that be?

Like the ocean currents, certain wind patterns make a difference in climate as well. Warm, moist tropical winds blowing from east to west are known as easterlies. They bring constant pleasant weather to the Hawaiian Islands and other tropical locations. These winds are also known as the trade winds. Long ago they helped power the sailing ships of traders. Winds that change direction twice a year are called

This map shows global wind direction. Easterlies move from east to west and are warmer than the wind that moves near the poles.

Monsoons happen in the summer. They bring heavy rain and often cause flooding.

monsoons. They often bring wet summers and dry winters to the regions where they blow. The most well-known monsoons occur in South Asia, Africa, Australia, and the Pacific coast of Central America.

COMPARE AND CONTRAST

Some winds are considered local and others are called global. Which kind is a sea breeze? Which is a monsoon?

ALTITUDE AND LANDFORMS

Altitude affects temperatures and, therefore, the climate. Temperatures decrease as height increases. For example, land high up on a mountain is cooler than land closer to the surface. Even in tropical areas the weather can be cool for people who live in the mountains. High mountains

The snow on the Rocky Mountains seen in this picture shows that the mountain peaks are colder than the land around them.

Altitude means height, especially height above sea level.

near the equator, for example, may have tropical plants at their bases but ice and snow at their tops.

Mountains can also block cold air from traveling into an area. This creates a warmer climate. Mountains keep some areas drier than others as well. They can block rain and snow from falling. The land on one side of a mountain may be much drier than the land on the other side.

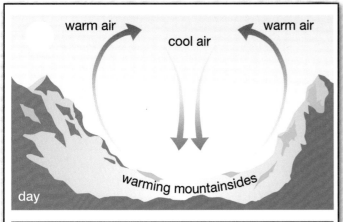

warm air   cool air   warm air

warming mountainsides

day

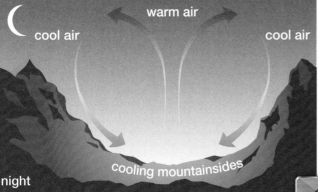

warm air

cool air   cool air

cooling mountainsides

night

By day, heated air rises along warm mountain slopes and descends into the valley. At night the opposite happens.

TYPES OF CLIMATES

No two places on Earth have exactly the same climate. However, individual factors combine to form several general kinds of climates.

Tropical climates are warm all year. Some tropical climates have a lot of rain. Others are dry. Tropical climates are found near the equator.

Subtropical climates are found north and south of the tropical climates. These have a greater range of temperatures than tropical climates. They also

The desert climate shown here is warm and does not have much precipitation or plant life.

may be humid or dry.

Cyclonic climates are found mostly north of the equator. In these climates, cold air from the poles mixes with warm tropical air from near the equator. This mixing often causes rain and snow. Cyclonic climates usually have warmer summers and colder winters.

This satellite photo shows two cyclones over the Pacific Ocean.

COMPARE AND CONTRAST
How is the weather in a tropical climate different from the weather in a cyclonic climate?

Polar climates are very cold. Snow and ice often cover the land. Some polar areas always have a layer of frost below the soil. This layer is called permafrost.

Highland climates are cooler than lowland climates on the same line of latitude. Highland climates have a great range of temperature between day and night. They tend to be humid and cooler than the lower lands nearby.

Within each of the general climate types there is a great deal of variety. For example, the island of Hawaii covers about 4,000 square miles (10,360 sq km) in the Pacific Ocean. It is near the equator so it has a tropical climate in general.

Like desert climates, polar climates have very little plant life.

COMPARE AND CONTRAST
Think about two different climates. How would daily life in these two climates be different? How would they be the same?

However, the eastern side of the island gets much more rain than the western side. If you climb one of Hawaii's mountains, you will find that the top of the mountain is cold and dry. Meanwhile, areas near the ocean are warm and wet.

This view from Mauna Kea in Hawaii shows how cold it is near the peak. At the bottom of the mountain is a warm beach.

Climate and Humans

Weather and climate affect people in many different ways. Weather affects what clothes people wear, how we spend our time, and how we travel.

Climate determines what kind of food can grow in an area and how much energy we use to stay warm or cool. Climate even determines where people can live. If a climate is too cold or too hot, too wet or too dry, certain animals and plants cannot survive there.

People can also have an effect on the climate. People burn fuels such

Most cars burn fuel that pollutes the air.

as oil and coal to run our cars and power our homes. When we do that, the fuels release gases into the air. These gases trap heat on Earth. Scientists think that this will make Earth warmer over time. This is called global warming. Global warming could lead to changes in our everyday weather and our climate. Storms may be more powerful, for example. Global warming can also cause polar ice caps to melt. This would cause sea levels to rise. Plants, animals, and buildings along coastlines would be in danger.

This huge hole opened up in the ice in northern Russia in 2014. Scientists believe it happened because of changing temperatures in the area.

GLOSSARY

atmosphere The air around Earth.

atmospheric pressure The weight of the air pressing down on Earth.

climate The usual weather in a place over a long period of time.

cyclonic A type of climate that mixes cold and tropical air.

desert A type of climate that is warm and dry with very little rain.

evaporate Change from a liquid into a gas.

fronts Borders between areas of cold air and areas of warm air.

global warming The rise in temperatures on Earth over a period of time.

hail Precipitation formed when water droplets freeze into balls of ice inside a cloud.

highland A type of climate that has a great range of temperatures between day and night.

humidity The amount of water in the air.

landforms Earth's features, such as mountains and plains.

permafrost A layer beneath the soil that is always frozen.

polar A climate that is very cold.

precipitation Rain, snow, or sleet.

subtropical A climate that is found just north or south of a tropical climate.

tropical A climate that is warm all year round.

water vapor Water in its gaseous state.

weather The daily state of the atmosphere in a given place.

For More Information

Books

Benoit, Peter. *Climate Change*. Brookfield, CT: Children's Press/Scholastic, 2011.

Close, Edward. *All About the Weather*. New York, NY: PowerKids Press, 2014.

Dawson, Emily. *Wet and Dry Places*. Mankato, MN: Amicus Publishing, 2012.

Gosman, Gillian. *What Do You Know About Weather and Climate?* New York, NY: PowerKids Press, 2014.

Lawrence, Ellen. *What Is Weather?* New York, NY: Bearport Publishing Company, 2012.

Ratti, Kristin Baird. *Weather*. Washington, DC: National Geographic Society, 2013.

Websites

Because of the changing nature of Internet links, Rosen Publishing has developed an online list of websites related to the subject of this book. This site is updated regularly. Please use this link to access the list:

http://www.rosenlinks.com/LFO/Clim

INDEX